Crowd Funding

A Comprehensive Guide for The Beginner

by Steve Woods

Illustrations by Shawn Raymond

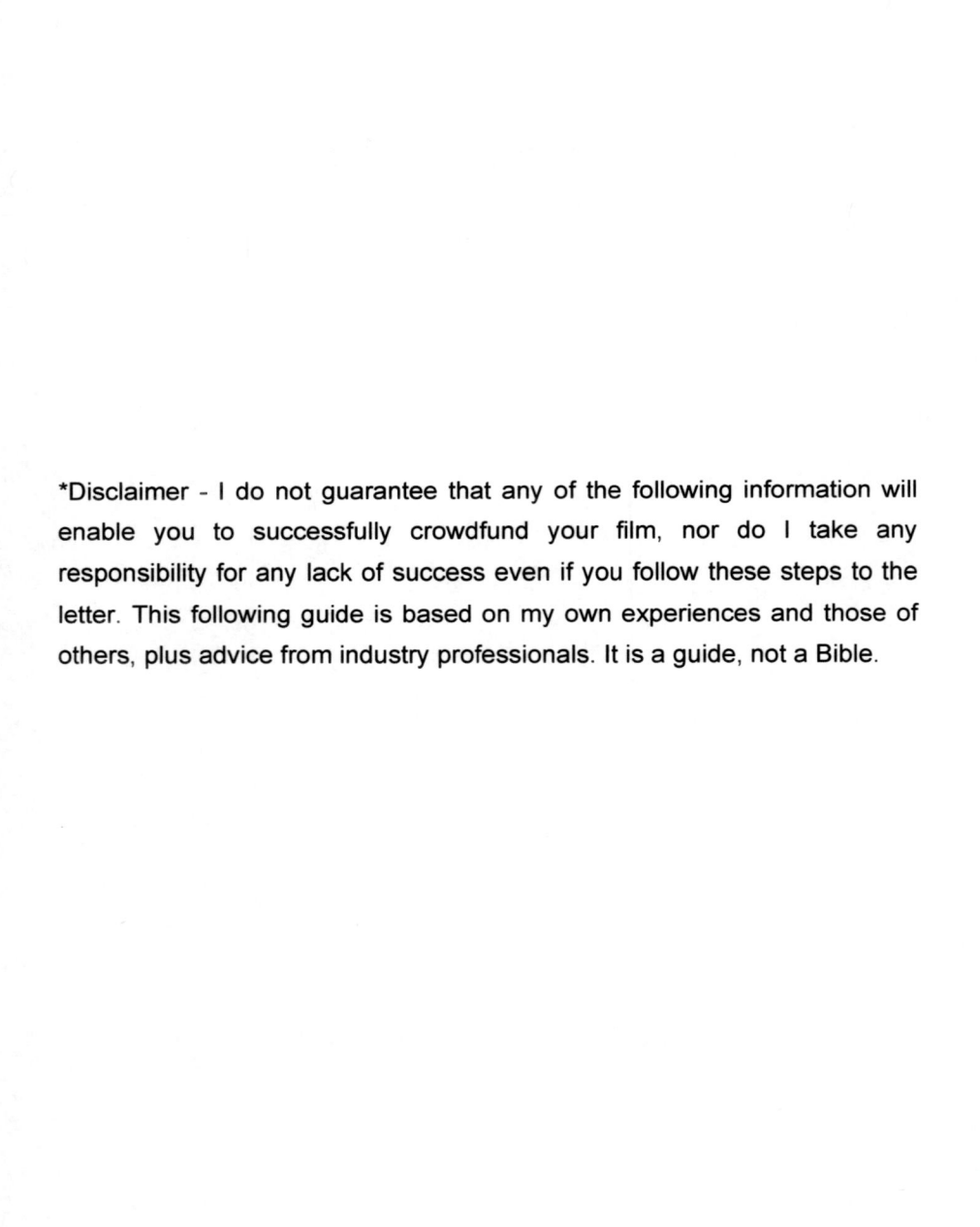

*Disclaimer - I do not guarantee that any of the following information will enable you to successfully crowdfund your film, nor do I take any responsibility for any lack of success even if you follow these steps to the letter. This following guide is based on my own experiences and those of others, plus advice from industry professionals. It is a guide, not a Bible.

First off, who am I and why should you read this? I'm an award-winning, trained actor with over 30 years of professional experience and a Masters Degree in film and TV production. As a director, my shows have won acclaim in London, Edinburgh and New York, and I've also been winning awards for my writing for over 10 years. Wherever I go and whatever I do, I'm always trying to learn something different, something exciting, something challenging. I'm obstinate, sometimes grumpy, opinionated, sarcastic and very hard to please. I only want and expect the best from those I work with, because I wouldn't dream of offering them any less myself.

I am not the fount of all knowledge, but I've had a lot of experience and I humbly share these (and those of some of my colleagues) with you so that you might...just might...manage to fund, shoot and distribute your own feature-length movie.

As a famous nun once said, "Let's start at the very beginning..."

What exactly is crowdfunding? Well, it's an online platform which allows you to pitch your project to (potentially) hundreds of thousands of would-be investors and donors. Essentially, you get your script, cast and crew together in one place and ask people for money - basically the Internet equivalent of standing on a street corner, rattling a tin and asking complete strangers if they could spare some coin. Now I'm all into donating to charity but, when you're faced with a dozen or more 'chuggers' (charity muggers) on a daily basis, you can end up keeping your hands in your pockets and your money in your wallet. It's all well and good telling people that Zach Braff or Spike Lee managed to raise hundreds of thousands of dollars in a matter of days - you're not Zach or Spike. They've got the provenance of a high-level track record behind them, have a huge fan-base and have dozens of high-level industry contacts and networks.

So how do you raise funds from strangers when you're competing against dozens of other film-makers, and no one's ever heard of you? As I said earlier, there's no guarantee to success, but the following suggestions and guidelines might just help you.

By the way, a word to the wise - if you're a first-time director, what are you doing? Think about it, you've never directed anything before, yet you're asking people to have enough faith in you that they'll give you their money. That, in my opinion, is unfair. Make your mistakes and learn your craft with your own money. Don't ask people to fund your screw-ups. I believe that crowdfunding exists for people who've spent some time honing their talent, not for those discovering whether or not they have any talent to begin with. Feel free to disagree with me, but if someone asked you to invest in a racehorse that had never raced, or a painter who'd never picked up a brush, what would *your* reaction be? Put in the groundwork, shoot a couple of shorts, learn from them and get yourself ready. This is for people making the next step, not the first one.

Finally, I appreciate that for many of you reading this, much of the information may sound like I'm teaching your grandmother to suck eggs, but I feel it is prudent to cover as many aspects of a crowdfunding campaign as possible. Most campaigns that fail to reach their targets are usually poorly organised as well as poorly marketed, so I admit to adopting a 'belt and braces' approach by providing as much information as I can.

PART ONE
BUILDING THE CAMPAIGN

Chapter One
Make sure you're funding the right project.

Not as easy as it sounds. You're convinced as a screenwriter, that your low-budget sci-fi/zombie/vampire rom-com is the best thing since someone started slicing bread, but I can assure you...it's not. I haven't read your script, but I'm willing to bet hard cash that it's not as good as you think it is. You will now disagree with me - fine...you're wrong. If you agree, then what are you doing reading this? Get back to that script and make sure the right people are giving you feedback - no, not mum/dad, boy/girlfriend, best bud'. They love you and will probably love your script - so they're not the best resource to use - join industry-level networking groups, let complete strangers give you feedback, and listen to that feedback - they're your potential audience after all.

Furthermore, even if the script is well structured and well-written, is it something that people will want to see? A 90-minute film about a guy sitting on a deckchair discussing 'Life' may be well written and well performed, but is it commercial? Will it sell? Will it make money? Personally, I don't believe that crowdfunding should be used for 'art house' film projects. Again, disagree with me as much as you like, I'm writing this for the guys and gals who want to move on to earn a living making well-received, audience-grabbing commercial projects, not pseudo-artists masturbating their own egos by crowdfunding a 4-hour snore-a-thon on the virtues of navel-gazing.

Having got that out of the way, here's a number of criticisms that have been levelled at scripts I've read over the years. Please look at each one and see if they relate in any way to yours.

1. There is nothing outstanding about this script, nothing that sets it apart from so many others.

In what way is *your* script different? In what way is your script *unique*? What is its ESP? The studios are always looking for that new voice in writing. Don't set your standards any lower.

2. The plot is clichéd and/or derivative.

Is *your* script 'by-the-numbers'? Is the story obvious? Don't go down the same tired old route that so many have taken before. Tread new ground whenever you can.

3. Too many typos and formatting errors.

Have you had *your* script proof-read for spelling mistakes - several times, by different people? Is it formatted to industry standard? There's plenty of free scriptwriting software out there. Don't look like an amateur by getting the basics wrong.

4. It's SO slow.

You've got 10 pages to make a first impression, not just on a reader, but your audience. Keep it moving, draw us in. After 10 pages, we should know who the protagonist is, and have some idea of what is ahead of them.

5. All the characters sounded the same.

Is your dialogue unique to each character? Can we tell who's talking just by looking at what they have to say? Write biographies for each of them, get to know them, and give them each an original voice.

6. I got confused - wasn't sure if it was a horror, a sci-fi or a comedy.

Of course there are film-makers who are able to weave multiple genres together successfully - Edgar Wright's 'Cornetto Trilogy' being a prime example - but you need to make sure there is a principal genre at the heart and running clearly throughout. If you're not sure of the staples considered to be *de rigueur* then you can always check online.

7. I didn't like any of the characters.

Whether your script is about Judas Iscariot, Adolf Hitler or Ed Gein, there has to be something compelling about your central characters. We, as an audience, have to want to know what happens. Even if your characters are the worst examples of humanity possible, they need to interest us in some way. Doesn't matter whether they're naughty or nice, we need to care about what they say and do. The same goes for the reverse - your good guys shouldn't be completely good, no person ever is.

8. I didn't understand what half the directions meant.

Don't go over-complicating things. Unless a specific action occurs, or unless a specific reaction is called for, or unless the location is relevant to what happens in that particular scene, you can pretty much go with the basics. Don't keep telling us what characters are thinking either - show us in their words and deeds. Show, don't tell.

9. The bad guys are all one-dimensional.

This goes back to #7. Just because a character is the antagonist doesn't mean they shouldn't be as well developed as the 'good guy'. There's a reason why Judas betrayed, a reason why Hitler hated, a reason why Gein killed. Their motivations came from somewhere - there is always a thought before an action. Always.

10. It's just not ready. It feels half-done.

If someone reads your completed script and goes away thinking it's an inept first draft, you're in trouble and you won't get a second chance. The script is the foundation of your project, which is why it needs to be rock solid. And there is a simple and reasonably inexpensive way of achieving this. It's called 'coverage'.

'Coverage' is basically a 2-page report on a spec script that breaks the story down into one page and gives a further one-page analysis. Studios will employ dozens of readers to critique the scripts submitted to them and the vast majority of execs won't read the script until it's had a favourable coverage report done first. Now, there are more readers than there are vacancies at the studios, so there's a glut of freelancers who operate outside the studios, but deliver to a studio standard, offering their services for very reasonable prices.

Getting this service done for your script is a must for anyone who has written a screenplay and believes that it is great, but is too close to the work to have a valid, unemotional opinion. To find an experienced reader to provide coverage, there are a number of websites that can help. Post a little notice on one (or all) of them and write something like...

"Independent film company with funding needs readers for coverage. Pay, £40 for 90-120 Page Script. Please submit a sample of your work via PDF files only to..."

What will happen is that dozens of up and coming writers/consultants/readers will respond, allowing you to pick one (or two, or three) to give you unbiased and impartial feedback on your script. What's more, if you offer the amount suggested above and they take it - you're getting a studio service for a third to one quarter of what it would normally cost. If only one of them suggests a problem with your screenplay, ignore them. However, if all three spot the same issue, then it's time for a re-write. Once again, I know you believe your screenplay is great but, you are too close to the project and need a non-emotional professional reader's opinion.

Now, picking the right project to crowdfund isn't just about making sure the script is up to scratch, or even that your project has commercial appeal, which begs the question...what IS the right project?
Truth is, there's no correct answer to that question. All sorts of different and wholly unique film ideas and projects have achieved success in terms of crowdfunding and many of these have gone on to be seen by people around the world. They either had a brilliant idea, or brilliant casting, or brilliant marketing. A select few, had all three.

Here are a few pointers to finding or developing the 'right' project...

1. Have a small cast.

Seriously, don't go for a script with a dozen or more speaking roles. If you do, then you face more complicated shoots, more need for rehearsals, more catering costs, more travelling expenses, more costumes, longer stints in the make-up chair, etc. Not to mention spreading your funding more thinly in salaries, more contracts to write up and check, and generally more headaches all round. If you think you have a great script but a large cast, look to see where you can merge characters together and shrink that demanding cast list.

This also includes large crowd scenes. I'm sure you'd love to have armies of zombies charging over the hill towards your hero, or a night-club full of young-bloods surrounding your heroine before she struts her stuff, but how are you going to pay them? I appreciate you've a lot of friends that will do this for free but, according to the laws in the UK, film extras are not counted as volunteers when it comes to the NMW (National Minimum Wage). By law, they have to be paid, and it doesn't even matter if you've got them to sign a waiver - the law is the law. Plus, how many release forms are you going to have to print out and get signed? What sort of refreshments are you going to provide? Will every extra get a copy of the film as payment for services rendered - how much more work are you creating for yourself? Think carefully before you include crowd scenes in your film, they may cost you more than you think.

2. Use few locations.

Again, try and merge scenes and dialogue wherever you can in order to keep the number of locations to a minimum. Think what an impact "Twelve Angry Men" still has today, and that takes place all in one room. Taking into account that it was originally a stage play, try and imagine your script in a theatre - how many scene changes would you need?

Every new location requires more permission slips, more release forms, potentially more Public Liability Insurance, higher transport costs...well, you get my drift.

Furthermore, if you feature a car, well-known location, corporate logo, branded goods, you could face an injunction from the copyright owner. As such, there are very few reputable producers or distributors who will touch your film for fear of the possibility of copyright infringements contained therein. If there is a recognisable brand or logo in your film, you could be signing the film's death warrant if you don't have the relevant permission.

3. Modern day.

By setting your film in the modern day, you save a massive amount of your budget by not having to hire in period costumes, set dressing, props and any other number of considerations. Furthermore, you're probably not going to have worry about allocating part of the budget to VFX shots or rely heavily on Special Effects either. Sometimes, for gun shots, scenic details or specific characters these skills are necessary, but unless you can get hold of a CGI wizard for peanuts or a prosthetics and pyro-technician for half a sandwich, I'd advise against going 'full Ferengi' or 'full Tron'.

4. Keep It Simple, Stupid!

Lastly, avoid car chases, collisions, crashes and explosions. Unless these are handled by an experienced, professional and JICS-registered stunt coordinator, who knows how to work action sequences for the camera, these kind of scenes invariably end up looking pedestrian and amateurish - not to mention the fact that scenes like these can be bloody dangerous and expensive. 'Action' sequences can also have an impact on the amount of insurance you have to pay, in case something goes wrong.

Even hand-to-hand combat and gun-play can look and feel out of place if they're not handled by someone who knows what they're doing. Plus, how many low-rent 'gangster' films are out there right now, flooding the market? Think outside the box and think how else you can create the action and drama without blowing something up or punching someone in the face.

If you go for a script that needs only a small cast, set in three or less primary locations in a modern environment, with little to no VFX or SFX, you're making life for yourselves a lot easier as well as saving money - money that could easily benefit your project in other areas.

Some filmmakers will try to argue that this approach somehow stifles their creativity, but I would argue the exact opposite. Keeping to a small cast in a select few locations forces you to be more creative and actually make more of the limited surroundings, as well as allow more time with each actor to help truly develop their characters.

At the end of the day, we're all striving for longevity in this game, so it would surely be foolish to hamper any possibility of such by making potentially ill-advised budgetary mistakes that could easily be avoided. Aim to move yourself forward one solid step at a time, and you increase the chances of there being another film waiting to step into.

Chapter 2
Make sure you're working with the best.

Ok, so you know someone with an HD camera and he knows someone with a microphone - but are they the best? Do they share your passion? Will they work as hard as you? It's all well and good 'keeping it in the family', but this is business.

How many low-budget films have you seen where the director is also the writer, producer, star...maybe even the editor, cinematographer, VFX supervisor and composer as well? The opening titles and closing credits just seem to have the same name(s) scrolling past all the time. Either that person doesn't know how to delegate, or trust his/her colleagues, or they're letting their ego get in the way...or they're Robert Rodriguez.

I mean, how many highly-experienced, highly-talented 'stars' are capable of that? Even with the millions of dollars of support and safety-net they command, how easy do you think doing all of that really is? And, is that ONE person the best choice for ALL those different disciplines? There's just no need for just one person to do ALL of that. Get some perspective - if you want your film to be the best it can be then I reiterate, get the best people for the job. And that's not always going to be you.

I strongly believe that the first person you need to recruit is a producer, and a hungry, determined one at that. Your producer needs to understand what your script needs in order to refine it, they need to understand budgets, how to assemble the most talented and enthusiastic HoDs, how to arrange a shooting schedule, how to manage contracts, and how to motivate everyone during pre-production and the shoot itself. They need to be a bulldog when negotiating and a diplomat when compromising. They need to be that unique blend of therapist and drill sergeant and, of course, they need to have your back. Most importantly, they need to be connected - no good if they're super organised and yet no one's heard of them - they need to have their fair share of industry credits too.

Now it's time to get a director on board. That, of course, may be you, it may be your producer, or it may be a third individual. I'm choosing to go with the last option so that we can fully explore as many different areas of responsibility as we can.

There's every chance you've already worked with a director whose style and approach is just right for your project, or perhaps your producer has a couple of names in their little black book that might be suitable. Or, you may decide together that bringing on board someone completely fresh and outside your current circle of contacts is the way to go.

Either way, you as the creator of this project need to have absolute trust and faith in their abilities to not only interpret your work beautifully and elegantly, but also to bring those brilliant and magical little touches that you hadn't even thought of.

But while you may be the designer and engineer of this film, it is the director who's going to pilot this thing, and it's (s)he who will ultimately decide on the HoDs to whom (s)he will delegate much of the work. Your director needs to understand how actors work, how dialogue is paced, how certain sequences will work together, how to shoot or frame particular shots, how to ensure that every angle is covered, and how to bring all the disparate elements together into a seamless whole. Once you hit the shoot itself, it will be your director 'calling the shots', so choose wisely.

The next big gun you want to hire is the production manager or coordinator. This is the individual who will calculate your budget, right down to the amount of fuel a mobile generator might need and, supervised by the producer, will make sure you stick to it. They can then become the production coordinator or Unit Manager and organise the shoot, ensuring that everybody is where it should be, when it should be there, and for no longer than it's needed. They have to be level-headed, calm under pressure and meticulous in their approach. When your location is ready, the set is dressed, the costumes fitted, the lights are on, cameras are rolling, actors are rehearsed, and the director's calling 'Action!', it is because the production manager and unit manager have made it happen.

If you can find one that has experience as a line producer as well, then you're onto a winner. Preparation is key when building a crowdfunding campaign, and bringing a production manager on board is an intrinsic part of that preparation.

Working in partnership with your director, bring on board your DoP, or director of photography. This is where you can collaborate with someone who can master the intricate and demanding shots that you and the director want, and if you 'shop around' you can easily recruit someone with a lot of their own equipment, potentially saving you thousands. You may end up paying twice as much in salary, but you'll save at least two-thirds of your equipment budget. What's more, the added benefit of using someone with all their own kit is that they will immediately know how to use it as well as be aware of any niggles or idiosyncrasies inherent in each piece. Make sure you check out their showreels and watch as much of their work as possible before you sign them on.

The same can be said of your sound designer who, these days, will comfortably double as your sound recordist and even sound editor as well. I bet your new DoP can not only recommend one, but recommend one with more kit than you'll ever need. The director of photography and sound designer will also have people in mind if there's any budget for assistants, so try and leave a little wiggle room for them to bring their team on board.

The last HoD that you should recruit prior to any crowdfunding campaign is the casting director or CD. This is the individual who will make initial approaches on your behalf to key cast. Here in the UK, we have the Casting Directors Guild (CDG) and they produce a list of members which should help find the right one for you, assuming you don't already know one.
If not, check out other low-budget features on IMDb and see who cast their key actors. Look for CDs that have worked with 'named' clients at least once and who have half-a-dozen or more credits to their name. Actors' agents tend to shy away from micro-budget features (as there's little in it for them), but if they're approached by someone with a growing reputation, you're in with a real chance of landing the talent that will help bolster your film's credibility and spearhead your marketing campaign.

With your various HoDs in place, you now have the core personnel needed to make your film a reality. It should be these department heads that recruit the necessary support teams that will assist them during production. Allow them to delegate and bring on board the people they know and trust, and your pre-production schedule should move forward without any major stumbles. Encourage your various departments to talk to each other and ensure that everyone understands their specific areas of responsibility.

Chapter 3
Assemble the best cast

Let's face it, at the end of the day, having put all this hard work into a (hopefully) great script, the last thing you want to do is put it in the hands of a rank amateur.

As I write, there are as many students training to be actors as there are actors already working in the business. In other words, the market for talent has reached saturation point. Tough for actors, but great for filmmakers because now you have a huge pool of talent to fish in.

But here's the kicker, the vast majority of low-budget film-makers are stuck in the mindset that 'good' actors are too expensive or, worse still, that their mate Barry can play the bad guy, "because he looks the part." If you've got a great script and a talented crew, doesn't your film deserve to have the best possible cast as well?

A director friend of mine, having studied at a prestigious film school and made several shorts, had an opportunity to direct his first feature on a budget of £150,000. He still managed to recruit British actors John Simm, Philip Glenister (Life on Mars) Ashley Walters (Top Boy) and Kevin McNally (Pirates of the Caribbean) as his leads. They all agreed to work for Equity minimum because they believed in the project. The director is now working on his 6th feature with a budget of £5 million.

Examine the figures for a moment. Here in the UK, we have some well-known soap operas such as Coronation Street, Eastenders and Emmerdale. They're broadcast up to four days a week, every week, every year. The biggest names and most popular characters are earning in the region of £150,000 per year - that's about £3,000 per week. Or, to look at it another way, you could employ a nationally-recognised TV actor (with thousands of adoring fans) for an entire week of shoots and comfortably pay what they're already used to earning - £3,000. Ok, you might have to sweet-talk a couple of them, or get rejected by others, but I assure you that you can find reputable, credible 'named' actors who (depending on the quality of your script) will give you what you want and need both in terms of performance and marketability. However, if you're still struggling to land your big name, then there's a little extra you can offer to entice them in - it's called Deferred Payment. It works like this...

You approach say, Danny trejo to shoot 5 days for your post-apocalyptic flick, and he agrees, but for 15k, a third of your budget. Your response should be to offer 5k upfront and the remaining 10k to be deferred until the film makes profit.

He's more likely to agree because he's still getting some cash up-front, with potentially more to follow. Benedict Cumberbatch (Sherlock, Star Trek 2) recently signed up to act in a short film which was hoping to raise a budget of £25,000 through crowd funding. Once his name was attached, the campaign raised in excess of 3 times that amount! Mark Gatiss (Doctor Who, Sherlock) has also signed on and completed a crowdfunded short film which, again, comfortably exceeded its target once he was on board. I could cite dozens more recognisable 'named' actors with very current, on-going careers who have graced the set and made an impact in many crowd-funded projects, both short and feature-length. You really can get some great names involved in your project, but they've got to want to be involved. The dialogue, the concept, the characters, the story are all areas of exploration for an actor, so make that journey as interesting as possible. You're not going to pay them Hollywood money, so there has to be something irresistible in the project itself.

The last little trick you can employ is 'Points'. 1 'point' is 1 percent of the gross profits earned by the production company responsible for making the film. You offer the 'name' a percentage of the profits - if there are any - and I'd still advise you to keep this type of offer as low as you can. You're not going to make a lot of money out of your first crowdfunded feature, so don't go giving away what little you might have. Aim between 5% to 10% (for a BIG name) and you should be ok. It's still a gamble - so much of film-making is these days - but with an offer of cold hard cash up-front (with the potential of more to come, plus a percentage of the profits), there are many actors with a recognisable international profile who'd consider what you have to offer - as long as the project is worth considering.

Don't waste your script/project on a cast with little or no accredited training - they will add nothing to the project, whereas a 'named' actor not only brings years of experience, but also public recognition that will help boost your project through funding and distribution. If you want people to give you money, especially in this fierce economic climate, then you better give them some bang for your buck!

Once you've landed your 'name', then audition for the other roles. A listing on Spotlight, posted by your CD and giving descriptions of the characters, and making it clear that Mr(s) X is already on board, will garner you some great results. Your CD will then arrange somewhere for auditions and meetings to take place and where you can film the readings. A script is sent out to the actor with their name printed across every page (bottom left to top right) as a faint watermark in a 20-point simple font (like Arial). This lets the actor know the script is meant for them alone - a polite nod to their status.

Film every audition, 'named' actor or otherwise, for future reference. This may cost a little to set up and run, but the rewards will be worth it. Then simply repeat this process until you have the cast you want/need and they've all signed a letter of intent. This is not a legally-binding contract, but a letter stating that should you meet all the agreed conditions, they in turn agree to play the role indicated in your film. They should also agree to be involved and cited in any and all marketing concerned, including your crowdfunding video, but we'll go into more detail later on that one.

Quality, 'named' actors will boost your credibility and thus your chances of raising funds, and they're not impossible to find - you've just got to look for them and bait your hook with something appetising. Remember, always aim high - never settle for second best.

Chapter 4
Working your budget

Simple question - how have you worked out your budget? Many first-time film-makers make the mistake of plucking a figure out of thin air, then allocating a portion to each department. Wrong. You have to discuss each department's needs with the relevant HoD and assemble the budget accordingly, adding at least 5% as a contingency or emergency fund (in case of re-shoots, etc). You need to know where every penny is going and why it's going there. You must know the budgetary needs and restrictions of each department, and still find a little wiggle room...just in case.

The professional way to budget is simply delegate the responsibility to your Production Manager who should know where best to spend your money so that it gives the optimum return in terms of talent, crew, locations, etc. And the PM will start with working out your Above-The-Line and Below-The-Line costs.

The above line costs cover the writer, producer, director and principal cast. The below line costs cover everything else. And there's a lot to cover - DoP, sound, hair, make-up, wardrobe, music, equipment rental, location expenses, props, catering and marketing to name but a few.

This means that you must keep the above line costs to a minimum. In other words, you're not going to earn that much out of this project at all. If you had any dreams of living the high life once you've secured your budget, then burn those dreams now. At best, you should look to cover your rent for 3 to 4 months, so you have some measure of security, but no more than this. You'll earn your big money out of the returns, so don't get greedy up front.

Take a look at the rental catalogues for equipment-hire companies and you'll see a lot of great kit, but the costs can seem off-putting. These costs however, are the rates charged to production companies and broadcasters with solid, guaranteed budgets. In other words, the equipment rental company will charge as much as they can because the person on the other end of the line is some PA or runner without the authority to bargain better prices. The PAs simply get the best kit they can from the cheapest (standard rate) supplier. You, on the other hand, can and should haggle for just about everything. The question you should be asking these companies is not "How much is X?" but "How much *discount* can I get on X?".

Most people don't like haggling for money-off deals as they feel embarrassed. Don't. The movie industry wouldn't exist without the ability to haggle, negotiate, barter or trade.

Here are a few tips to help you on your way to getting cheap stuff cheaper, and cheaper stuff free.

1. Ask.

The sad truth is, most people don't even think to ask for money off, or free stuff. They see the price, they pay the price, they never question it. Don't sit there believing "They'll never go for it". You won't know until you ask.

2. Avoid emails.

Talk to people. Use the phone. Write a letter. Make an appointment. In other words, make an effort and make it personal. The people you're approaching get emails by the dozen every day. You're going to achieve a much higher level of success by using a more innovative and personal approach.

3. Get to the point.

Make your offer short and sweet, clear and concise. Don't make promises you can't keep either. Briefly introduce yourself, ask for what you want and what you're prepared to offer. Haggle. Get a deal. Thank them for their time - move on. Make it easy for them to deal with you, and you'll end up getting a better deal.

4. Don't get cocky.

Don't spin your film to be the Citizen Kane of its generation. Even if it really is that good, producers and suppliers will have heard this hyperbole before. And don't expect people to call you until you've established some rapport with them. It's as much about having faith in you as well as the project. So if you come across as some big shot with a sense of entitlement, you'll turn people off. Be professional, not arrogant.

5. What's their base line?

If you're renting say, a camera and lenses, you can rest assured that it's costing the supplier no more than one-third of what they're charging you. So you should be able to offer to pay two-thirds up front, assuring the supplier a profit while you land a one-third discount. For little extras such as bonnet-mounts or monitors, suppliers would rather these items were rented out for a little something, rather than sitting on their shelves earning nothing and gathering dust. Try and bulk up your order with as many little extras as you can.

And it's ok to tell potential suppliers that you have a small budget. In fact, you're more likely to get a good deal if you state your case and make a sensible offer. And, whatever you do, return the kit on time and undamaged. Don't screw up a good thing for other film-makers.

Budgeting is also about networking. It's about having a list of contacts you can go to whom you know/hope will help you out. It's about asking family and friends (and others) if they know someone who has the prop/vehicle/location you need. Budgeting is about focusing on the absolute essentials first and foremost, then looking at the little luxuries and extras once the fundamentals have been taken care of.

At the end of the day, what's the worst that can happen if you try and haggle for some discount? They'll say 'No'. That's it. The Heavens will not rain down on you, life on Earth will not end, and Existence as we know it will not collapse into the black abyss of Nothingness. And even IF all that does happen - it's probably due more to Armageddon than your negotiating skills. What *will* happen is that you'll move on to haggle with the next contact and learn from whatever mistakes you might have made. Budgeting doesn't always mean doing things cheap - but it does mean doing things smart.

Chapter 5
Create a following.

This is the most crucial area of your preparation. Even if your script or concept is utter garbage, a big enough following will garner some financial support.

It doesn't matter that your last short film got 237 'Likes' or 82 'Views'. That's an insignificant amount when it comes to crowd funding. It's great that people liked what you did, but you need more. Going back to the charity box analogy, how many people walk straight past without donating for every one person that does? Maybe a 10 to 1 ratio, maybe higher? And that's for a recognised charity that saves dolphins, or lives, or the planet...or something.

Let's say that you need £60k to make your feature film - that works out at about 2000 people donating an average of £30 each. In order to get those 2000 to donate, you need to have had 10 times that amount visit your crowd funding campaign and, in order to achieve that much traffic, you've got to have made your campaign known to about 10 times that number again - that's 200,000 people that need to have heard about your film in order for just 1% to donate. So, how do you get people to follow you?

Well, you've got to be interesting for a start. As I said earlier, you're competing against so many other crowdfunding campaigns out there, that you've got to make sure yours stands out from the rest.

But in tangible terms, you've simply got to use all the different resources at your disposal; Facebook, Twitter, website, a regular blog, etc. I'm not talking about bombarding people 24/7 with posts asking people to 'Like' you, I'm saying that this is where you need to encourage and entice potential donors and investors into taking the journey with you. It's about selling yourself before anything else. Don't 'hide' behind your project, stand tall and let people know who you are and what you're about. People need to engage with you before they engage with your dreams. Here are a few avenues to explore.

1. Website.

Have you got one yet? Is it clear, concise, un-muddled and easy to navigate? Look at the websites of other independent film-makers - what do you like about these sites? Could yours benefit from similar improvements? Your website is the front door to your film-making empire, and it's got to be as inviting and welcoming as possible. Keep it simple, keep it clear, make it interesting.

If you haven't got a website yet, then they're easy enough to get up and running. Most of us know someone who can throw a rudimentary site together but even if you don't, website designers and builders are simple to track down online. Use a resource like Craigslist or Gum Tree, post an advert asking for website designers to create a bespoke website for £100. Offer to promote their services on your site, check out the offers you get, find the one that suits you best, and don't settle for second best. Only pay them once your site is just how you want it. Designers use your site as an example of their work in order to gain better paid jobs, so use your haggling skills to get the best deal you can.

2. Facebook

Nearly everybody and their dog has a Facebook account, and so should your production company. You're looking to create an online presence so, even if you hate the idea of FB, use it to your advantage. Build a rapport with people, engage them in conversation, ask questions. The first rule in getting people to 'Like' you, is to get them talking about themselves. Psychologically speaking, they feel as if you are genuinely interested in what they have to say, and so will respond favourably to you.

Talk about what short films you've shot in the past, post photos and clips from previous projects, ask for feedback and take that feedback graciously, even if it's negative. A friend of mine used to do clown shows for little kids, and whenever one of them started to get a bit mouthy during his act, he'd get that kid to help him out. Suddenly, that kid feels like he's the star of the show and behaves himself. The same goes with negative feedback - someone trashes your movie, not necessarily because it's bad (although it may well be), but because they're challenging you. They're seeking attention and want you to respond to the gauntlet they've just thrown down.

Accept the challenge gracefully, ask for their advice, discuss the issues with them. Now they feel as though they're collaborating with you - they have the attention they seek and feel as though their opinion is worth something. Once you have them doing clown tricks beside you in front of the other kids, they'll follow you anywhere.

3. Twitter

This is about building a following with the 'right' people. If you're an impoverished film-maker, there's little point in asking other impoverished film-makers for donations, they've most likely got their own projects to fund. By all means, interact, network and connect with other film-makers, but they're not going to be any sort of significant revenue stream for you. What you need to find is a 'sponsor'.

Most people outside of your circle won't have a clue as to who you are. You may possess awesome talent in your field, but until that talent is recognised and talked about outside of your circle, pretty much no one cares. Who'd heard of Neil Blomkamp before Peter Jackson became his sponsor and mentor? After garnering rave reviews for District 9, he's now released his second feature, Elysium, and is riding high. You need to find a 'name' that will support you too.

It has been demonstrated recently that a single promotional Tweet from a mid-tier actress in a UK soap opera will prompt over 1000 visits to a website (or crowd funding campaign). That could mean several thousand pounds in donations. Go through your address book, ask your friends, family, colleagues and see if you know anyone with access to a 'name'. And who knows, if you make the right contact, they might not only help to promote your project, but also appear or put you in touch with someone who could boost your cast list.

4. Write a blog.

Sites like Tumblr, Reddit and WordPress are really strong ways of letting people know who you are and what you're about. A 300-word article, once a week, shouldn't be any real hardship so, again, engage with people. Talk about your favourite films, genres, actors. Talk about your ambitions, the state of the independent film business in the 21st Century, the latest piece of kit, and so on. Choose topics you have a clear understanding of, or that can be easily researched. Slowly build up a following of interested and engaged readers. Link other writers' blogs to yours, build a network - post links to your website, FB page and Twitter - and vice versa. Encourage people to connect with you by sending out a regular newsletter. Make it so that subscribers need to supply their email address - which means you are not only continuing to engage with your audience, you're gathering direct contact details for later on. Keep all these email addresses in a separate folder on your website's email account, and it means you have an immediate database of contacts ready to approach when your campaign launches.

These social networking tools will prove invaluable if used effectively. If you don't pester people, or gather their contact details in an unscrupulous manner, after 6 months of steady work across these different platforms you should have been able to build a strong and diverse following that feel as if they know you and, more importantly, can trust you. These followers will be the foundation upon which you build your campaign and spread the word.

Creating a solid following is going to take you and your team a good six months, so plan well ahead. Join as many filmmaking groups on FB as you can, subscribe to other blogs, tell people about yourself and past projects and they won't just see you as someone after a quick donation.

Build a relationship. If your initial approach is "Hi, I'm X and I need some money," then you'll get nowhere, fast. You wouldn't go up to someone in a bar and ask them to come straight back to yours for some bouncy-bouncy (unless you're 5 years old and have an inflatable castle). You'd charm them, flirt with them, allow them to get to know you - building a following is pretty much the same thing. It's a slow burn - make it count.

Part Two
Launching The Campaign

Chapter 6: Rewards

In terms of your crowdfunding campaign, the 'rewards' are essentially the gifts or incentives that you pre-sell for each donation. These can start from as little as £1 (or Dollar, Euro, etc) and then go through a number of levels until they reach the highest donation for that campaign. This can be as high as £25,000, but unless you're a Hollywood player aiming for a seven-figure budget, I'd advise against looking quite so greedy.

Your rewards have got to be pitched in such a way that they maximise the potential for income, while minimising the cost to the production. When looking at the different types of reward you can offer for your project, your first thought should be "What can I offer that costs me little or nothing?" Usually, it starts off at a simple 'thank you' or a name-mention on Facebook or Twitter, but what should you offer next, and how much for?

As is so often the case, there's no straight answer to that. I would suggest however, that you make each level of reward not only as attractive as possible, but also as personal to the project as you can; and there's one major reason for doing it that way - people don't usually invest in a film because of the nature or scope of the rewards offered, they invest because of the film itself. The rewards, incentives or perks are simply a bonus, a way of saying thank you.

Again, I understand that there may well be many out there who'll disagree with me on this subject, but just think about this for a moment. Would you invest in a painter just because someone offered to send you photographs of the finished work? of course not - you'd invest because you either had faith in the project, faith in the artist, or you just loved paintings. Well, the same goes for crowdfunding campaigns - make the rewards as personal to the project as possible.

For instance, does your film require period costume? Yes, I know I advised against that direction earlier, but I bet some of you won't listen. If so, then one of your rewards could be signed copies of the original designs. Is there an action sequence? Then offer signed copies of the storyboard. Have you got a 'named' actor on board? Then offer signed headshots or stills, etc. If people are going to invest in the project, then give them a little piece of it.

Other rewards should obviously include a copy of the finished film, but that doesn't mean you need to sit up all hours of the night burning a whole bunch of DVDs and post them halfway round the world. You need to minimise the cost of the rewards as much as possible, so offer a free DOWNLOAD along with JPEGS of the cover artwork. If you're having original music composed (much less expensive and far more personal than paying through the nose for the rights of already published material), then offer a free download of the soundtrack, and so on.

Most crowdfunding sites offer a range of about a dozen or so levels of reward, but you really don't need more than 7 or 8 to get yourself started. You can always add new levels and new rewards later, but for now it's best to keep it simple. One good thing to be aware of is that the average donation works out at around the £20 mark, suggesting that's the figure most people are comfortable parting with. It makes sense therefore to tailor your most accessible rewards around that level - £15, £20, and £25 becoming your most popular donation levels. That being the case, if a £25 donation gets you a shout-out on Twitter, a free download of the film, free artwork, and a free download of the OST, then it's not a huge leap to ask £35 for a couple of signed cast photos on top, or to then ask £50 for adding on a signed storyboard to the list. Making small but significant increases in the cost of the reward, yet adding value for money as well as personal/collectable items, leads to 'impulse buying'. Supermarkets have been doing similar things for years - 20% extra in a tin of something, but only a 10% increase in cost, for example. You don't NEED extra, but you see a saving and buy on impulse. Or those two-for-one offers - again, you don't NEED two of that product, but you perceive a saving and so buy on impulse.

By employing an intelligent marketing and sales strategy with your rewards, you can not only fund your film but you're also selling memorabilia that will captivate and please your customers.

What about tailoring rewards to suit specific markets or trends? For instance, your writer could offer a feedback service on other writers' scripts for £120. That's not only a fair industry rate, but you're also offering everything else associated with that level of reward as well - shout-out, free download, free signed photos, free storyboard, free OST, etc - what's not to like?

Your Production Designer could offer a one-hour Skype chat to a prospective student designer, or your director might present a seminar to an amateur film society. Think outside the box, consider ALL your talents and resources.

Many campaigns in the past have offered rewards such as an 'executive producer' credit, IMDb credits, and even a percentage of any of the film's profits. Whilst I agree with these rewards in principle, I urge anyone considering offering such incentives to really think them through first. In terms of the industry paradigm, the executive producer is the individual responsible for raising the funds for the project. They are well-versed in all the intricate legalities associated with financial investment and will invariably handle a portfolio of known cash-rich investors and contacts, and have the wherewithal to draw up a rough draft of the Offering Memorandum - the UK term for an investment prospectus. They will have built up strong professional and (in a lot of cases) personal relationships both with serious investors and distributors. Do you really want to hand over all that credit and status for a small investment? Furthermore, what level of return do you think your film will generate - is it enough to give away percentages?

Consider these figures: When a film obtains a cinema distribution deal, the box office will retain an average of 60% of the ticket price. Of the remaining sales revenue, most distributors will take around half, leaving the film company with just 20% of the original ticket price. Out of that, the film company will then have to cover any and all deferred payments previously agreed with cast and crew, plus any percentage deals struck in order to secure the involvement of some individuals. If you then have to return investments and the investors percentage, there's not going to be a lot left for you to enjoy after 2 years solid, hard work.

I'm not saying don't go down this route when it comes to drawing up your rewards, just be very careful when you do. If you haven't got watertight contracts, if you screw up your figures in some way, if your lack of experience disables this aspect of funding in any way, you risk creating months of headaches, face the possibility of legal action, and potentially ruin things for both future filmmakers and investors alike.

There are so many ways in which you can incentivise your donors to part with their cash and, I'm sure if you sat down with your production team, you'll come up with much better ideas than mine. The key is to make it personal to the project, attractive to the donor, and inexpensive to supply.

Chapter 7: Campaign Video and Poster Design

Your campaign video is possibly the single most important aspect of your crowdfunding campaign. Statistics show that campaigns with a video are up to three times more likely to raise funds than those without one. It's a tool for engaging all those potential investors, and helping those investors and donors better understand your project and the people behind it. This is your online pitch, the investors' window into your world, and it has to grab their attention from the get-go.

In order to create the desired impact, your campaign video is going to need attention to detail and careful planning throughout, as well as employing a fairly simple structure - much like a movie script.

1. Intro

People make snap judgement calls on a daily basis; the first time they meet you, shake your hand, talk to you - they judge your hair, your smile, your clothes...and there's a simple reason for this - we're all programmed to find out in as short a time as possible, whether or not we're going to 'like' something or someone. It's a standard defence mechanism that we've carried over from our prehistoric ancestors, and we all do it. The same will happen with your campaign video - it will be judged in the first 30 seconds, so you need to make them count.

Tell your audience who you are and what they're going to be viewing. Maybe you've shot a teaser trailer as part of your campaign project - good, but introduce it first then, once it's done, explain clearly what you're after. 'Top and Tail' the teaser with the face behind the project.

2. Credibility

It's all well and good believing you have a great idea/story, but investors or donors need to believe in you first. Be professional, polite and to the point. Clarity is the key here, so don't warble on about inconsequential matters - clearly explain what your film is about, and what you hope to achieve. Be real, and be realistic.

3. Rewards/Incentives

These are usually listed alongside your pitch document on the crowdfunding page, but it's not a bad idea to also let the audience know a little about what you're offering. be enthusiastic without seeming manic, and don't make promises you can't keep.

4. Wrap It Up

This is your Clarion Call, your rallying cry, your 'Braveheart' moment. Be passionate, be persuasive, be professional and, above all, tell people just how important they are to you and how much of a difference their contributions will make to your project. Convince them one last time what a great movie it is, and how you are just the right person or team to bring it all to fruition.

Watch as many other crowdfunding videos as you can, especially those associated with successful campaigns. What do you like about them? What works, and what doesn't? How could you improve upon them?
Move things along as crisply as you can by keeping your video to 3 minutes or less. With cable and satellite TV providing us with hundreds of channels, not to mention thousands more available on the Internet, attention-spans in this new Digital Age are shortening. Don't bore your audience by over-staying your welcome.

Try and include info graphic illustrations to highlight certain bullet points, as well as stills, designs and other visual material that might enhance the presentation.

Finally, even though you're surrounded by a full crew, ask someone else to shoot your campaign video. not the teaser part, obviously, but try to get someone with an advertising or marketing background to bring his or her own vision to this part of the project. And while we're in that vein, allow the director of the campaign video to recruit their own producer and cinematographer too - treat it as though they're your advertising company - give them a brief, see what they deliver. This technique creates the opportunity for an impartial approach from a new set of eyes, hopefully furnishing you with a fresh perspective, whilst at the same time, delivering a professional and targeted sales pitch.

Now, as any of my friends will tell you, I'm no graphic designer, so don't expect any jaw-droppingly stunning design advice here. However, I do have a few tips and themes that I've gleaned from past experiences and research, which I think are worth sharing. The first one is obvious...

1. Get a graphic designer

Yep, it's as simple as that. Just as you would if you were branding any other product, you employ a design professional to do what they do best. Seriously, the number of times I've been presented with quite accomplished films, yet the DVD and poster design looks like it was handled by a five year-old, is staggering. This will be the first image that audiences will see of your project - get it right.

2. You're not creating art

Oh, stop complaining - yes, I'm fully aware that movie posters have become art; you only have to look at the work of Saul Bass and others to understand just how beautiful these designs can be - but that's not the purpose of the design. The DVD cover and film poster exist for one reason, and one reason only - to promote sales. It doesn't matter right now what beautiful ideas and unicorns made of sherbet you can cut-and-paste within your frame, if they don't sell the film, they're pointless. The poster is there to put bums on seats, not to make bedroom walls look cool. use your poster to promote, not decorate.

3. DON'T think outside the box

Understand the generic conventions of your film, and examine how other films have stuck within those conventions when designing their poster. That's what you need to do. Follow the layout set down by thousands of film-makers before you - don't try to re-invent the wheel, or be too clever or 'arty'. Audiences know what they like and, more importantly, they like what they know. Stick within the design conventions of your genre, and you won't go far wrong.

4. Stand out

A single, clear, recognisable image will always be stronger than a mish-mash jumble of fonts, pictures and explosions of light and colour. You shouldn't include portraits of your cast - unless you have secured a 'name', in which case, go for it! - just try and evoke a memory, a feeling, a sense of what your film is about. A bold title, a clear image, a strong tagline - the rest is smoke and mirrors. And don't over-complicate things by using an entire palette of colours either. You've got to catch the eye of a passing stranger and draw them in - they've got to want to know more. A fussy, confused poster with a rainbow of different colours and fonts actually pushes people away.

Chapter 8: USP and ESP

Your Unique Selling Point and your Emotional Selling Point are two different things entirely, but will often work together. Your USP should be obvious - it's that aspect of your project that makes it unique, different from all the others, that makes it stand out from the crowd. "Outland" with Sean Connery is essentially a "High Noon" remake set on a space station. "I, Robot" is essentially a murder-mystery where an Artificial Intelligence may or may not be the culprit. "Beowulf" is a 1200 year-old poem shot with 21st Century animated 3D. We are all familiar with these stories or genres, but the way in which they were told made them different...unique.

What's special, different or unique about your project? What sets it apart from the crowd? When chocolate and chillies were first brought to Europe from the New World 500 years ago, their taste was seen as revelatory. The Royal Courts of England, France and Spain had never experienced anything like that before and they quickly became 'de rigueur' across the kitchens of noble houses in Europe. At one point, sugar and spices were worth more than gold. These days, I don't know anyone who hasn't eaten either chocolate or chilli as least once in their life, but in the late Fifteenth and early Sixteenth Centuries, any dish that included just one of those ingredients was considered to be unique. That being the case, you need to find the chilli or chocolate in your project.

Is your film a comedy? Then perhaps you could include a couple of pages of riotous dialogue. Is your film 'high concept'? Then find a way to highlight just how innovative your musical-in-outer-space really is.
Whatever you've got that separates you from the run-of-the-mill, shout about it.

Your Emotional Selling Point is a different animal altogether. It's the beating heart not only of your campaign, but of the very project itself. There may be many reasons why this film means so much to you now but, right in the beginning, there was one driving, irresistible siren-call that tempted you above all others. What was it about the story/character/issue that compelled you to write/direct/produce this film? Is it the same reason why others got on board? Then that's your ESP, because that's going to be the same reason why potential investors will 'buy in' to your project and campaign. It's not necessarily about tugging at heartstrings, and it shouldn't have anything to do with the technical side of the filmmaking process (no matter how creative and skilled those various departments are), as that would come under USP.

No, this is about that gut feeling, the core, the soul of your project. Sell that, and you sell your campaign.

Chapter 9: Distribution

Getting a distribution deal prior to landing your funding is both difficult and not always a guarantee of success. However, should you find yourself able to jump the myriad obstacles and fight past the ever-increasing number of 'gatekeepers' to find yourself negotiating a potential distribution deal - well done, you've got further than most and have put yourself in danger of generating revenue!

The bad news is that there is little likelihood any of the major distributors will even see you, let alone offer you a deal. However, the good news is that there are dozens of reputable, independent film distributors and agents out there who are open to approaches from low-budget filmmakers.

With any luck, your producer has probably worked with some of them and can open that door for you and your project.

Prepare your team, get your 'pitching hat' on, make that appointment and give it your all. What's the worst that can happen? They could show you the door. Fine, look for another one. They could say, "Come back when you've got funding, or a 'name'." Now you've got someone prepared to look at your project once you've met their conditions. Or, they could sign a letter of intent, and your crowdfunding campaign gets a massive boost.

Either way, you'll have gained some invaluable industry-level feedback, you'll have practised your pitch technique, you'll have learnt a lot more about how the industry works, and you'll have secured a great contact for the future. Here are a few things you'll need to have in place when discussing the future of your project with potential distributors.

1. Rights

Are you the copyright holder? It can all seem somewhat daunting, discussing the murky world of rights and ownership, but it's of vital importance that you know what rights you have, and what rights you're prepared to sign away. You will only be able to secure distribution and screen your film in public if it is 'cleared' first. This means that you need to have full written permission to use everything and everyone that appears in your film. Your script, any products, logos, stock footage, images, even the fonts used in opening titles and closing credits - all have to be cleared for use. Then there's music, sound effects, locations, actors, the names of your characters...Yeah, it's headache-zone central but, as Douglas Adams would advise, don't panic. There are plenty of online resources that will help you pull everything together.

2. EPK

Your Electronic Press Kit is a must-have when talking to distributors. On a single disc, you should include your trailer, a full list of credits (with a spell-check on ALL names!), production stills, a synopsis, any poster or DVD cover designs, and any press releases or press coverage that you might have. This way, distributors or sales agents have all the necessary media information immediately to hand.

Also include details on the length of the movie, year of production, original format (whether you shot it on 35mm, 16mm, Digibeta, HD, etc), the logline, any co-production or record label deals, copyright details, URLs including links to your website, reviews of previous productions, and contact details for your producer and director.

You might also wish to tell potential distributors of any festivals this movie (or others you've made) has played at, or been selected for, including any prizes or awards won. Include a separate file for music cues with a list of all legally-cleared or commissioned music with details of the rights obtained.

Finally, a shooting script or dialogue list (which you will have been expected to encode on the Master Copy) allowing for an accurate record of the scenes and dialogue. This makes translating into other languages or adding subtitles easier and cheaper for overseas markets as well as audio- or visually-impaired audiences.

Once all of the above has been assembled on one disc, make absolutely sure it plays on both a PC/Laptop and a regular DVD player. You're looking to make life as easy as you can for these people because, that way, reaching a decision in your favour becomes a little easier too.

3. Production Stills

You should have included a whole range of these on your disc, but it's always good to include a few printed copies with the EPK as well. During the shoot, or while you're putting the teaser together, or on a day organised solely for this purpose, get some portrait- and landscape-sized shots together. Distributors love visual material, it's grist-to-the-mill for them. try and get a mix of relaxed and action shots; solo, double or multiples. Give the distributor as many choices as they feel they can handle. I usually get my stills photographer to take between 1500 and 2000 during the course of a day's filming, but I'm not suggesting you copy that many onto your EPK disc - 50 or so should be enough to get the ball rolling. And don't forget, production stills are also a must for your FB page, Twitter and production blog.

4. Bios

Going back to that idea of people investing in you before they invest in your project, write up some biographies on key cast and crew. This information can then be used for advertising, marketing and press releases by a distribution company or sales agent to create interest or 'buzz' about your film. The more materials you are able to provide about your project, cast, crew, and the making of the film, the easier it becomes to sell on to stockists, suppliers and, ultimately, end-users.

Before I close this chapter, I just wanted to go back to a point I raised earlier. I mentioned that the screens that show your movie will keep 50-65% of the ticket price before the distributor takes their 35-50% of what's left, leaving you (or your company) with 17.5 - 32.5% of the original sales figure. And, as I said earlier, this is where it's possible for the production company responsible for making the film in the first place to enjoy some serious returns. However, you need to understand that the production company will earn the smallest portion of the pie...every time.

As you continue to make bigger and better movies, so your share of the pie will get bigger but, for your first couple of films, don't expect to get back much more than 15-20% of the retail price. Landing a distribution deal prior to funding isn't necessarily key to your campaign's success and, to be fair, is something of a long shot. But this doesn't mean you shouldn't go for it, nor does it mean you shouldn't learn as much as you can about all the potential revenue streams available to you. Do some research, look at other low-budget independent films and see what deals they struck through online retailers, cable TV, pay-per-view, etc. Aim to do even better with yours - consider all the markets and make sure you appeal to as wide an audience as possible

Chapter 10: Logline and Pitch

1. The Logline

The logline is essentially the short, attention-grabbing description of your film. It's not to be confused with the tagline, the punchy one-liner you see on posters at the multiplex - "You'll believe a man can fly!" or "In space, no one can hear you scream." Think of the logline as flirting - you're saying, 'here it is, want some more?' You're giving just enough to whet someone's appetite, create a desire, the motivation to want to know more and, because the people reading your pitch are invariably busy, your logline has got to give them all the relevant information in the shortest yet most captivating way possible. I've been writing them for years, and it always needs careful consideration - loglines can make or break interest - so take your time getting it right.

The logline needs to contain the following information - the protagonist, what makes them interesting, their objective, the obstacles in their way, and the resolution. The standard structure therefore would read something like, "An interesting character has a goal, but in their way stand many obstacles to overcome and, in so doing, they learn something valuable about themselves."

Yeah, it's formulaic, but it's a formula that's proven to work. It distils your story down to its essence, keeps it clear and direct, and helps the reader understand at first glance just what's on the table.
If people can tell right off the bat what your film is about, they'll be more inclined to read on, and read more favourably.

2. The Pitch

The craft of the one-page pitch is every bit as demanding a skill to hone as the logline but, thankfully, there is also a formula for this as well. You need a beginning, a middle, and an end. That's it, folks, that's all you need. A beginning, a middle, and an end.

George M. Cohen, the famous American music hall performer and impresario described the classic 3-act structure thusly; "Act 1, stick your guy up a tree. Act, throw stones at him. Act 3, get him down from the tree."

Your campaign pitch needs to follow the same simple structure that Cohen described. The first act of your pitch is the introduction to the project, the principal players involved, the journey you are about to embark upon, and what's at stake (why it's so important to you). The second act should detail the various obstacles in the way of your project, how you intend to overcome them, what you need the funding for and how you'll spend it, plus any other helpful information such as set and costume designs, proposed locations, and the themes and styles you'll be employing in order to tell your story. The last act will detail your principal cast, any distribution deals, festivals entered, and any other news about your project that may have the 'wow' factor.

Don't make each section too long or complex. Use bold paragraph headings, exciting stills and dynamic language. I know I keep saying this, but ENGAGE your audience. The pitch is not just there to inform, it's there to sell! Whatever information you include in your campaign pitch, make sure every line of text is designed to create desire. be careful though not to go overboard - a pitch that relies on hyperbole can be just as off-putting as a pitch that under-sells itself.

Now that you're ready to launch, we can focus on maintaining the campaign - this is the nail-biting, nerve-wracking climactic final act and so, to go back to those old film quotes..."Fasten your seat-belts, it's going to be a bumpy night."

Part Three

Maintaining The Campaign

Chapter 11: Tools In The Toolbox

We're going to be speeding through these sections and, like a well-oiled campaign, we'll be done in no time.

There are two ways to run a successful campaign - raising the necessary funds all in one go, or spread out over a number of smaller campaigns. It's entirely your choice and both methods have proved to be equally successful - so how do you choose which route is best for you?

1. The Single Campaign

Have you got one driving concept that will take your project from inception to delivery in one fell swoop? Have you got a 'named' actor that will figurehead your project and attract donors just by their profile? Is your project light on VFX, low on cast members, only requires a couple of locations? Then maybe there's no need to over-complicate your life or campaign by chopping it up into bite-sized pieces. The best route for you probably be the one-shot campaign which will nail that funding in a sprint finish.

2. The Multi-Pronged Campaign

Have you got three or more set-pieces requiring multiple cast members and/or extras? Does New York get over-run by a plethora of giant spiders? Will you need several months in post-production knitting it all together? Does your project contain a number of different talking points that could appeal to a variety of specific demographics? Then perhaps a piecemeal campaign might be best for your project, allowing for a more targeted approach.

This decision, like all other major decisions regarding your project has to be discussed thoroughly and objectively with all key personnel, including principal cast. Will you be asking them to commit over a long period of time, whilst allowing them to work on other projects in between, or will you want them to give a solid concerted burst of energy and focus, exclusive to all else?

I put it that way because that's exactly what your cast and crew need to understand. The piecemeal path allows opportunity for other work in between each little burst of filming, so no one involved is putting themselves under any undue stress or pressure by working on your project - you can literally tailor your campaign and shoot around their timetable rather than push them to adhere to yours - which is going to be demanding.

But giving it everything you've got over a short 6-week period (thought by many to be the optimum limit for single campaigns), then you can gain momentum, ride the wave and drive it home in one fell swoop. But you've got to be super-prepared, have every single resource ready to go and be 'match fit' because you're going to be sat in front of that monitor, or on that phone, or knocking on doors for 6 hours a day, 6 days a week, for 6 weeks. It will be frustrating, it will be frenetic, and it will be fatiguing.

Whichever route you take, make sure it's in the best interest of the major players involved, and make sure you keep on top of it all the time. Even those fragmented campaigns need managing and maintaining in order to be effective.

Social Media

1. Facebook

Whatever you do, don't go spamming every contact, every group, every passer-by with robotic posts on a daily basis. By now, you should have done all your networking, primed all your resources, forewarned every friend that you're about to launch, so there's no need to continually pester them. A fresh and unique post, twice a week, is quite enough. Mix things up a bit - post a headshot and short bio of your 'named' actor one day, then an update of how well you're doing on the funding front the next. Make sure your posts are upbeat and informative; maintain that level of interest with your followers and do your best to persuade them to spread the word.

2. Twitter

Much the same goes for this networking tool, but you need to have got on the good side of some big hitters, as I explained earlier. The word needs to be spread far and wide with this one - a short message, along with the URL to your campaign, sent from a popular individual on Twitter will attract attention to your project.

3. Blog

By now, you should have posted 50 or more times on your blog, accumulated 1000+ followers and linked it to as many networks as possible. You'll have made your posts as informative as possible, and as researched and captivating as you can. You'll have linked it to your website, you'll have copied links onto FB and Twitter, you'll have shared the link with all your email contacts and asked them to share it with all their contacts, and so on. I really meant it when I said this was going to be hard work.

4. Other websites

All those other bloggers, those film sites, those reviewers, those critics, those whose opinion means something - those are the ones you'll be hitting with press releases and EPKs for the next 6 weeks. All those Internet contacts that you've followed, interacted with, shared opinions and links with, added to your web of contacts - now's the time to fully exploit those relationships. Offer to give interviews, inform them of how well your campaign is going, send them exclusive stills, make the act of supporting you as easy as you can. There's an old sales-training expression I've heard many times, "People only buy from people they like." So, make sure people like you.

5. Family and Friends

If you do your research on successful campaigns, you'll find that the vast majority have two vital aspects in common - they raised 20% of their total through family and friends, and had achieved half of their target in the first third of their campaign. Think about that for a minute - if you're running a 60k campaign over 6 weeks, then you should be looking at 12k of donations coming from family and friends, as well as hitting 30k inside 2 weeks. It's a tall order, but it's the path to success.

This is one of the major reasons why you need to plan ahead - it's time to reacquaint yourselves with all those relatives you only see at Christmas or Thanksgiving, and get in their good books. Visit all those rich aunts and uncles, get to know their rich friends, get your personal network right behind you and supporting you all the way. To put it bluntly, during your months of preparatory work, you need to find out who your real friends are.

5. Local/National Press

Contrary to popular belief, the press can be your friends. Local press love stories about celebrities, especially if said celebrity has a link to the local area. Look at all the different regions of the country your cast and crew hail from - write up individual press releases detailing how successful each cast/crew member has been, include a couple of stills (preferably with your 'named' actor), and give as much information about your campaign as you can.

Where I'm based in the UK, there are at least 3 weekly newspapers covering the 3 major towns, but not all 3 are owned by the same publishing group, so do your research and find out which publications are affiliated and which are not - that way you'll know who to target for maximum coverage.

Include a Q&A interview with the director, or the local cast/crew member and, if you've got one, comments from the 'named' actor. As before, it's about making life as easy as you can for those spreading the word on your behalf. My local rags have a combined circulation of roughly 100,000. If only 1% see an article about a project I'm involved with, that's upwards of 1000 potential new followers and donors. Multiply that by a dozen or more local newspapers around the country (based on principal cast/crew members), and you're starting to create real interest and a real following for your project.

The national newspapers are different - they deal with big stories and big names on a daily basis, so you need to have some serious, heavyweight bait on your hook to reel them in, but it can be done. If you've got an angle, something that'll help them sell papers, they'll talk to you. Maybe your 'name' has got a contact, or their agent knows a friendly journalist who might write a little article. The same goes for local TV and radio stations - arrange an on-air interview (pre-recorded or live) and plug away. Talk about your crowdfunding experience, how it's the future of independent movie-making, how you're taking on the big boys., and so on and so on.

I keep saying this, but it's true - look for every opportunity for putting yourselves in danger of raising those funds. Every person, every shop, every local business, local radio station, cable TV network and local or national publication is another avenue worth exploring and exploiting.

The Email Has Landed

This next technique may feel a little bit gimmicky but, if executed well, does work.

First off, you need to write a letter to all your personal email contacts (personal, not business) and ask them flat out to do you a favour. All you're asking them to do is...

1) 'Like' your Facebook page

2) 'Share' your Facebook page

3) Forward the email to all their personal contacts and ask them to do the same, including asking their contacts to forward it on again, and so on.

The success of the technique is reliant on how persuasive you are in your initial request, and that in turn is reliant on the strength of your fan base, but it really is that simple. Yet, at the same time, a delicate, complex and fragile strategy. In composing the content of your original email, you've got to address a number of different people, ask them to do a number of different things, and still make it feel as though you're talking to each person individually and only asking them for the smallest of favours. That's not easy, and you may have to re-draft the email several times before you've achieved the right tone and balance, so let's go right back to the beginning of the campaign and look at that section where we created a following.

Gathering in friends and family is easy enough, especially if you've reinforced each request via a personal email. If you've done it right, you'll have got your entire production team to do the same thing, thereby accumulating hundreds (if not, thousands) of personal contacts in your database.

Over the 4-6 months of your preparatory work, you should send out your initial email (starting the ball rolling) but follow up no more than once a month. All new followers on Facebook and Twitter should also be approached to see if they'd like to be on the 'newsletter' email list as well. Promise not to spam them, or use their details for anything other than your film. With each new email, give your ever-growing number of recipients the chance to unsubscribe (and a few may, that's fine), but also remind them to forward the email on to their personal contacts.

Through all your Twitter networking, your Facebook posts, your blog, your website, and those regular and informative emails backing everything up, you should be able to build up a database of contacts numbering in the thousands. The more the merrier, especially if they're legitimately harvested, because these contacts will now become your front-line troops in the email barrage.

When you actually come to launching your campaign, send out one final, persuasive call-to-arms email and ask everyone on your list to a) donate as much or as little as they can, and b) forward the entire email on to all of their contacts, asking them to repeat the process and so on.

Some of you may not like the concept of the chain email, which is why I said it was a delicate and fragile technique to employ. However, should you employ it to its fullest potential, the rewards can be quite staggering.

If, for instance, you and your team have accumulated some 2000 email contacts prior to launch, and only 20% respond to your requests, you've already raised somewhere around the £5-10,000 mark. Not bad. Furthermore, those 400 contacts have passed the email on to (on average) 10 contacts each, meaning that your message is now being read by another 4000 people. If only 5% respond favourably, that's another 200-odd people donating on average £25 each - that's another £5000 in the bank. So using the email method alone, working on low figures, and with no follow-up during the campaign, you can probably bring in about 10k of donations

Now what if...what if...those 200-odd strangers also pass on your email to 5 each of their contacts, and so on? The beauty of the chain email is that it has the chance to continue on and on until the campaign is closed. I'm not suggesting for a minute that the chain email can solely fund your film, or that the results suggested here are the top or bottom of the expected range. You might be able to bring in a lot more, or indeed, a lot less. It all boils down to the content of the email, and the reliability of your following. But get it right, and the sky's the limit.

So, what do you need to put in this 'magic' email that's going to get everyone banging on your door?

1. The Introduction

Be open and upfront right from the beginning. Tell them straight away that you're going to ask them for a couple of favours. You wouldn't normally ask, but this project means so much, you just have to give it a try.

Go on to explain that if they should feel uncomfortable in any way, they should just ignore the request and delete the email.

At this point, the recipient of the email is close to wondering how many laws this favour is going to break, and why are you involving them! Hopefully, when they read on and find that you just need them to click a button on Facebook and then help spread the word, they'll be more inclined to grant your request. Each time you ask your email contacts for a favour, make them think it's going to be a big deal, then land them with something a lot softer and easier to handle instead. It's a simple trick of emotional and psychological game-playing, but it can be effective.

2. The Request

Make it simple and make it clear. "I need you to do X please." Whether you're asking them to 'Share' on Facebook, Tweet something, spread the word via email or even donate, just ask, plain and simple. Include a link in your email to the various pages or sites you need them to go, tell them how much this project means, and how much their support could make a difference. You're asking them because they're a friend. Boost their ego, twist that arm, nail that support.

Get them to forward emails on to as many as possible, by making it a game or competition. Is your film about 'Urban Life'? Then ask your friends to forward it on to a dozen or more of their friends they'd choose as 'Homies'. Is your film about zombies? Then get them to recruit a post-apocalyptic team of zombie hunters, and so on. If you give them something else to think about when granting your request, they won't be focusing so much on what it is you're actually asking them to do.

Just like in the earlier chapter about perks and incentives, make the idea to forward it on as personal to the project as you can. Really push home how important, how life-changing, this project is for you, and how grateful you'll be when your friends fully support you.

3. The Wrap

Be polite, thank them for their time and apologise if they feel you've crossed a line. Always come across as humble and gracious rather than desperate or needy, as that would really kill your chances.

And don't forget, after your friends forward the email on to their friends, you'll be addressing complete strangers, so be aware of your language and tone. Be professional at all times - your friends will be impressed, and their friends will respect you for it.

Private Investment

Maybe you've decided that crowdfunding isn't going to bring in enough, or maybe you're thinking that you're ready to take on the next level of the game. Whatever your reasons, the road to private investment is a rocky one and should not be travelled unprepared or without an experienced producer guiding the way. There are so many pitfalls, so many contracts, so many legal and financial obstacles that to enter into any sort of financial agreement regarding your film demands expert support and advice.

However, the level of information and research required, as well as handling the questions most investors will ask, is all good training and experience for you as an independent filmmaker.

Now, most independent film investors don't actually do it for the money. They'll tell you that they are so they sound like they know what they're talking about, but they don't really. With all due respect, any investor in their right mind wouldn't touch a low-budget film with a 10-foot barge pole - there are so many easier ways of making money. So, when approaching an investor and dealing with their questions, don't forget that they will not only invariably be investing for the sheer fun and excitement of making a film, but at the same time, also wanting to look as financially smart as possible in order to justify their decision to invest. Your job is to help them look smart while getting them to accept the situation for what it is, to allay their fears, and remind them just how amazing working in the film industry really is.

There are no guarantees that you will ever find yourself in front of investors pitching for their business but, if you do happen to find yourself in such a fortunate position, they will want to know a number of key things.

1. What equity are you offering?

In other words, what do they get for their money? What percentage of your gross profits are you offering? Do they get a say in how the film's made? Easy enough questions to ask, but not always as easy to answer. Think long and hard about how much of your profits you want to give away, and whether or not you are happy for any creative control to rest in the hands of someone else.

2. How much will I make?

A lot of investors will be expecting returns of up to ten times their original input, but most realise they will see a lot less or even lose everything. You can highlight past success stories, you can quote statistics, you can even show comparisons with similar projects, but you can never offer a guarantee. Don't even try to. NEVER promise a return on someone's investment, because there's no way you can contractually live up to that promise. You can tell people you will do everything you can to ensure success, but you can never guarantee it.

Here in the UK, you can help offset some of the risk by offering to protect their investment via the SEIS/EIS UK Tax Credit schemes. It's a great way to crowbar potential investors into the party as a significant proportion of their investment is effectively insured against loss - however, it is still not a guarantee that your project will make money, just a guarantee that if/when it doesn't, they will not lose all of their investment.

3. How long will this take?

Investors don't just mean the film when they ask this, they mean the whole deal itself - they want to know when they're getting their money back - and truth is, it's going to take at least 2 to 3 years. You're going to need time for pre-production, principal photography, post-production, distribution deals, release, etc. If your project is looking at a pay-per-view or standard cable TV release, the returns may be sooner, but 3 years is still your safest bet.

4. Have there been other films like this? How did they do?

The investors are looking at like-for-like comparisons here. Similar films or genres, with similar cast/crew experience. How well did these projects do? Did they make money? In other words, can you demonstrate that you have a solid proposal based on the success of previous outings of other projects? And don't exaggerate here - by all means, show some films that have done well, but don't blow them up bigger than they really are - the investors will know that films can be risky and should do their own investigation into your figures. Don't try and tell them that everything in the garden will be rosy. Always be honest about your project's chances.

5. How much did these projects make?

This won't be easy information to find, so you're going to have to do some digging around. Many producers or sales agents won't even deign to give you an answer, but you should be able to make some educated guesses based on the info you do get and, if you offer confidentiality (other than sharing ball-park figures with your investors), you might even get full disclosure.

6. Can we see your accounts?

Investors need to ensure that you're not some fly-by-night snake-oil salesman who's going to try to rip them off, so hire a collection agent to collect all the revenue from sales on your behalf, then pay the investors in accordance with the deal signed. This way, you offer a secure and protected conduit through which the investors' input goes straight back to them before anyone else. It's nigh-on impossible to get ripped off this way, offering a level of comfort and security to 'nervous' investors. The short answer then is, yes you can see our accounts.

7. Do you have a detailed budget?

Yes, of course you do. The investors will want to make sure you've thought everything through, that you've covered every eventuality, that you've made allowances for re-shoots and pick-ups. You need to demonstrate that you can deliver this film on time and, most importantly, on budget. No one wants to throw you a financial life-line at the 11th hour, especially if you're sinking faster than the Titanic (the ship, not the film, natch!).

8. Who are you?

The investors will want to know your track record or that of the director, as well as any awards won. Don't bother boring them with whatever courses or training schemes you've completed, unless you were top of your class at NTFS or UCLA. Put together a sizzling showreel of your best work, as well as a short reel of any 'names' you've secured amongst your principal cast and crew. Everything you show the investors has to demonstrate talent, credibility and reliability. You'll never get another chance to bring investors on board if they see that you don't know what you're doing. When you make promises or bold statements, live up to them.

9. How is my investment protected?

In other words, what are you doing to not only ensure the film is completed, but completed to a high standard that will attract sales? Investors don't want to look stupid, so don't dither about or put a 'spin' on anything. Promise a completion bond, show all your prep' work, show your research into the market, and demonstrate that you have surrounded yourself with creative, technical and professional talent.

10. What makes your film unique?

This goes back to that section on your Unique Selling Point. The investors need to be reassured that you're following a well-trodden path, but they also want to see what makes your film stand out from others like it. What's going to make it stand head and shoulders above the crowd? What's the gimmick, the MacGuffin, the trick you're using to bait the hook? What's new and exciting about it? What's your 'Wow' Factor and will it sell tickets?

There will no doubt be dozens of other questions asked of you and your team, but those already listed will be the most important and relevant for the serious investor. If you've pitched well enough, and answered those questions comprehensively, there should only be a couple more to deal with.

What perks are you offering?

They're not talking about DVDs or crew T-shirts (but a memorabilia package is always a good gift for investors), they want to meet the cast, visit the set, arrange an audition for their daughter/niece/girlfriend, and they will want some on-screen credit. Some of these perks will be easy enough to organise and should be offered as standard to all private investors, but when it comes to exchanging roles for financial input, be VERY careful. Don't promise anything other than an audition for the person involved, and don't 'sell' a key role unless the actor suggested is competent enough to offer what's asked of them. Now is not the time to cut corners on the film's integrity.

The last question to be asked should come from you, and it's a simple one...

Are you in?

Festivals

There are only 2 valid reasons for submitting your film to a festival - to win an industry-recognised award, or to make a sale - anything else is just ego. That being the case, there are only 2 types of festival worth submitting your film to - the festivals with a prestigious reputation, and the festivals attended by industry buyers. To enter your film into a festival that does not have an A-list reputation, or is not attended by industry buyers is both pointless and a waste of money.

Furthermore, I would advise against entering your film into a festival that you, or a member of your team, cannot personally attend. So many lazy filmmakers just pop a DVD into a padded envelope, or upload their file, then wait for the news. If your film is accepted into a high-profile festival, then it's an absolute must that a representative of the production company is in attendance to talk to festival organisers, to address any queries from the Press, and to take the contact details (at the very least) of any interested parties such as retailers, sales agents, distributors and the like.

I'll admit that entering into the big festivals can be expensive, so choose the one that's right (and easily accessible) for you.

Your choices include (but are not limited to) Sundance, Tribeca, Toronto, Cannes, Berlin, Edinburgh and Raindance. Attending these festivals will be some 2-3,000 sellers but only 2-300 buyers, and the vast majority of those buyers will only be looking at acquiring the top 5% of those films on offer. The top 1% of those films will be the subject of bidding wars (great news for the filmmakers involved) but the other 99% will be pitching, cajoling, spinning and, in some cases begging for time alone with those very important buyers and they will have (at best) a 1 in 10 chance of securing a deal. The odds, I'm afraid, are against you. However, the work you've previously done getting your EPK together, as well as practising your pitch (keeping it as short and sweet as possible) will hold you in good stead, as will the following little tips.

1. Be prepared

Always have your press pack to immediately to hand, including your business card. I've seen so many inexperienced filmmakers successfully door-step a potential distributor, only to ask them to wait while they scoot off to collect their press bits and pieces. Naturally, the buyer (who never has time to waste) has moved on by the time the filmmaker has returned, and the opportunity has moved on with them.

2. Be polite

Don't bad-mouth ANYONE or their film as bad news travels fast. The last thing you want in a crowded festival hall is some irate filmmaker confronting you or your team about your inappropriate comments, or some buyer turning their back on you because you've criticised the film they've just bought. I think it was Sam Goldwyn who said something like, "In

Hollywood you can walk into a man's home, eat his food, discipline his kids, make love to his wife and kill his budgerigar, just don't criticise his film!"

3. Repetition works

If you're going to be talking to people about your completed film, then make sure you talk about it properly. Mention the title half a dozen times during your conversation, give buyers a couple of free tickets to the screening in an envelope with the film's title (and screening details) on the front. Make sure they know who you are, and make sure they know what you're selling. As I've said so many times already, be clear, be concise and engage your audience. And repeat, repeat, repeat the title.

4. Talk to the Press

On arrival at the festival's main reception desk, you'll be asked to sign in, you'll be given a little 'goodie' bag (map, timetable, promotional material, etc) and your ID badge or Pass. These usually come in 3 different colours - one for the filmmakers with an entry in the festival, one for Press and the last one for all the festival staff. Find out which colour the Press badges are and door-step as many as you can, ensuring you've got your promotional material at all times.

Remember though, nothing is ever 'off the record', and never respond to a confrontational question - simply thank them for their time and walk away, or answer a different question entirely. Politicians have been doing it for years!

Success!

    What exactly is success? People tend to confuse the word with fame and fortune, but it simply means reaching your goal or achieving what you set out to achieve, and that's make a film. If you have managed to put together a finished feature film, then you have been successful. It really doesn't matter whether or not it wins any awards, or whether or not it achieves any discernible sales - you have made a feature film, you're a success.

To build on that success, you must learn from whatever mistakes you might have made, you must listen to those you trust the most, you must seek out the advice of professionals. If you move forward on a new project without learning anything constructive from your last outing, then what's the point?

A couple of years ago, I was privileged to be on the set of War Horse as they were getting ready for a crane shot. The scene was due to follow a horse as it was being led along a track, then crane up and over an archway to focus on the soldiers and battlefield beyond. Just as they were about to start, Jan Kaminski (DoP) grabs a shovel or a pick (can't remember which) and begins taking lumps out of the ground with huge swings, then filled in the resulting hole with some water from a bucket. Spielberg couldn't figure out what Kaminski was doing and we all watched in bemusement as the admittedly zany DoP went about his demolition work. Satisfied with his labours, he shot the scene as he'd seen it in his head, opening on a (newly-created) puddle before craning up. It was a beautiful shot. In that moment, we all learned something about how a scene is viewed through a lens. There is always something new to learn.

That being said, what if you did win some awards, or make a decent financial return? In order to capitalise on that sort of success, you need to choose your next project wisely. Don't be swayed simply by the prospect of big money offers - most of the time they never come to fruition anyway - now is the time when you can afford to pick and choose, and, if you're really lucky, you can afford to be very choosy indeed. Here in the UK, an independent filmmaker used to budgets no bigger than £300k, has just signed on to direct the first two episodes of the next series of Doctor Who, with Peter Capaldi as The Doctor. Ben Wheatley's films may be known only to a select and discerning few outside the UK, but stepping up to the next level now means that his work will be seen and enjoyed by millions around the world on primetime TV.

For me, as I've mentioned before, success is about longevity. Plan ahead every step of the way, not just in terms of the individual projects themselves, but also in terms of your career path. You've just shot a feature film, so use it at the very least as a calling card - get a showreel to agents, managers and producers. Make sure the industry knows who you are and what you're capable of. You already know that you can crowdfund another film if the agents don't take the bait the first time around, so consider that option a safety net. The best way to work the industry is from the inside and, once you're 'in', the opportunities to network and promote opportunities are almost limitless.

Over the next twelve months, I will be working as a crowdfunding mentor and producer on 3 different projects, each of which is looking at a budget of £250,000, and I'm still looking at new ventures beyond those. Maybe they'll be successful in terms of financial returns or critical approval, or maybe they won't - there are no guarantees in this business - but either way, I will be doing what I love doing best. Who knows, maybe I'll get to work with one of you guys one day?

As I said right at the beginning of this little book, I am not the fount of all knowledge - 30 years in the game and I'm still learning something new every day. However, I hope that the vast majority of you who've read this will find something new, useful or inspirational within its pages. I wish you all the very best in your future careers and, should you ever need any further advice or support, you can always drop by for a chat on Facebook. I'd love to hear from you.

Take care, and all the best.

Steve Woods

CPSIA information can be obtained at www.ICGtesting.com
Printed in the USA
LVOW12s1914230614

391261LV00027B/1240/P